ANOTHER ARM

of the

HYDRA

The Undefined Life

JILLIAN MAI THI BURKE-EPPERLY

BALBOA.PRESS

A DIVISION OF HAY HOUSE

Balboa Press books may be ordered through booksellers or by contacting:

Balboa Press
A Division of Hay House
1663 Liberty Drive
Bloomington, IN 47403
www.balboapress.com
844-682-1282

Because of the dynamic nature of the Internet, any web addresses or links contained in this book may have changed since publication and may no longer be valid. The views expressed in this work are solely those of the author and do not necessarily reflect the views of the publisher, and the publisher hereby disclaims any responsibility for them.

The author of this book does not dispense medical advice or prescribe the use of any technique as a form of treatment for physical, emotional, or medical problems without the advice of a physician, either directly or indirectly. The intent of the author is only to offer information of a general nature to help you in your quest for emotional and spiritual well-being. In the event you use any of the information in this book for yourself, which is your constitutional right, the author and the publisher assume no responsibility for your actions.

Any people depicted in stock imagery provided by Getty Images are models, and such images are being used for illustrative purposes only.
Certain stock imagery © Getty Images.

Interior Graphics/Art Credit: Jillian Mai Thi Burke-Epperly

Print information available on the last page.

ISBN: 979-8-7652-3689-5 (sc)
ISBN: 979-8-7652-3691-8 (hc)
ISBN: 979-8-7652-3690-1 (e)

Library of Congress Control Number: 2022922177

Balboa Press rev. date: 12/07/2022

Necessary Legal Disclaimer:

Follow me on Social Media:

https://www.facebook.com/jillyjuicellc2

TABLE OF CONTENTS

ACKNOWLEDGEMENTS

I would like to thank both John Oakes from England and Audrey Stewart from Dundee, Scotland for their contribution to the research and development of this amazing innovation. If it was not for John's wit and intelligence as we were bouncing ideas off of each other, I would still be looping in numbers, letters, and symbols.

If it was not for Audrey mentioning the hydra at the most appropriate time, I would not have put it all together. I appreciate both their contributions along with everyone who contributed their support and stories and watched my rants and raves as I kept discovering new and brilliant thoughts harvested from the energy of everyone. Even my critics contributed to this book.

As I close this chapter of my life, I also would like to thank my husband Stanley Jason Epperly for his never-ending patience and once this book is done, I promise to go fishing with him.

11/15/2022

CHAPTER 1

I AM JUST ANOTHER ARM OF THE HYDRA

I AM JUST ANOTHER ARM OF the hydra, which is a "mythical" creature based upon the microbial life in all water sources, including your immune system. Hydra grow, evolve, and change with the conditions and when hydra arms become damaged from environmental conditions, another arm grows acclimating itself to the new environment. Hydra are literally parasitic, even to themselves, and with their ability to adapt, can live in other creatures hosting them, in all types of conditions, making them the most immortal or adaptable species on Earth.

Just like me, the last 48 years of my life have taken on the characteristics of a hydra flitting from place to place, identity to identity, family to family, friend to friend and I never felt like I could fit in. I was not meant to fit in nor bred to fit in. The very basis of my childhood and immigration status came from one identity, ripping away one culture such as Vietnam, to then try to develop my own following or leading in a diverse melting pot called the United States of America. My life at this point is undefined, and relative to the environment

I live in, is indefinite. If the conditions drastically change for whatever reason, my life is still indefinite.

Indefinite life or undefined life means there are no parameters defining one's life to be a number value or a compartmentalized thought process. There are no politics, no religions, or scientific dogmas I subscribe to defining what my life means or what anyone else's life means. I have no sexual orientation, though I am married, but with all intents and purposes marriage is a business contract defining division of labor and financial agreements with a few rolls in the hay and respect is paramount and love is desired but not required. When you think about it, I was bred to be and am a hydra within a tardigrade of a system meant to evolve and change. If I resist the changes, I die. If I adapt to the changes, I live. I consider myself lucky I was not programmed to be anything but an academic in the proper context. This is my story and my perspective of the world I live in.

The other day in the Summer of 2022 I was racking my brain about how I was to introduce myself to give you some background of my basis of experience. In spite of its unconventional nature, it is not to be rejected since society has many ways of learning. I was taught the academic way in my childhood, and certain schools programmed children academically with less emphasis on the arts or sports. I was taught teachers in their respective subject matters are to be taken quite seriously and never to be challenged. In addition to teachers, I also was taught that anyone in authority regarding a belief system was also to be taken seriously and never questioned. Society has so many layers and layers of participation that it is easy to find authority within each layers and become a follower. Leaders and followers are a dime a dozen if some offers something "new" or "different" to say, or maybe all the leaders and followers in our society are selling the same thing repackaged.

In my case, I was a Vietnamese Adoptee with extreme health issues, and one of which was pneumonia which developed into a misaligned immunological system affecting my behaviors and learning capabilities. You can imagine what a new parent with scientific methods of the day to program their child had to deal with, and on top of that, deal with a child with literal "monsters" growing inside of her rebelling against medicine, rules, and extreme programming. I discovered later, the use of strong anti-biotics, popular at the time, contributed to my health issues developed later on in life which eventually, turned into an anti-biotic allergy when used on other infections later on, coloring my perceptions of the world. If you cannot join them, or fit into society, then my mantra was to beat them at their own games.

My rebellion eventually led me to stay in a variety of "reformatory" institutions, such as the Girls Center in Contra Costa County, the children's shelter in San Jose, California, and Martinez, California, and the juvenile hall in Martinez where I spent 30 days after shoplifting. After leaving home at 15, attending alternative high schools, and living in many foster homes and group homes, I married at 18, divorced, and finally decided to make my own way. That was just the tip of the iceberg.

If anything, my experiences in the institutions exposed me to the different gangs in Northern, CA like the crips, bloods, Norteno's, Surreno's and white supremacists and got in fights, and ran away from some of those institutions and became extremely angry at the world. You can imagine how much that shaped my perspective on the world; there was no way I was going to live a traditional lifestyle. That did not stop me from trying, however, when rebellion is instilled in you coupled with extreme intellectual academic stress, I can see why Charles Manson (cult leader) or Ted Kaczynski (Unabomber) had an issue with Academia and society as a whole. Luckily, I did not turn out like them, but my government, at the time of the Jilly Juice in 2018, certainly thought that was the direction I was headed. My saving grace, I purged the demons of retribution a long time ago throughout my life, determined I was not to be another statistic found on the local news.

In my opinion, Kaczynski and Manson were programmed to be counterculture, much like I was. Was it the initial intention, who knows, but the "right" kind of programming on the wrong kind of person will have unintended consequences or intended consequences. I will never know the truth but both perspectives of intentional and unintentional, are relevant. In other words, science is all about vast amounts of experiments representing a multitude of factors, so the projected intention has a mostly predictable outcome in a controlled environment.

Fast forward to 2022, and the Jilly Juice recipe purging out a lifetime of bad experiences, trauma, and then memories, for me to strategize the Jilly Juice Journey, subconsciously I had to dig deep into traumatic memories. Consciously, I also had to remember all the jobs I was fired from or quit because of health issues or lack of assimilation issues. I had to remember the countless colleges and classes and self-help courses based out of San Francisco, CA, the land of the reformed "cults". I had to remember the suffering from moving place to place, state to state, my travels to China, and living in Hawaii, Mississippi, Washington, and of course all over California.

I have been exposed to movers and shakers in Hollywood and media moguls, not just a T.V. doctor, and also those in the finance world when I was a nanny in my 20s. I hung out with people older than me who had vastly more knowledge than I, along with different boyfriends who were seasoned in their high-level jobs, or classes, or meeting people in the adult education world in Sacramento, CA who were also part of the tech industry. I absorbed so much information, and desired to understand everything. I felt I had to make up for not graduating high school with only a GED and two ASVAB scores with two different jobs in the military.

At some point, after all that memory and antibody purging feeling the symptoms of evolution, I realized I must understand who my parents were because I had extreme hatred towards both of them, my mom in particularly because of her Avant Garde child rearing methods. I did try to relate to her, in the late 1990s and early 2000s but the scars were there, deep inside. I also realized later, with how sick I was, if it was not for her methodologies, would I have fought so hard to live and survive? If it was not for her methods of boundaries, hard lines, and tough love, I would have probably died a long time ago. Tough parents and families can either make or break a person. In this case, she made me, in her image. I love and respect you mom, despite it all.

Developing something so innovative and capable of evolving and uncovering our society's secrets truly took facing my own demons around my entire background. Despite not being classically trained to stay within traditional lines, I didn't have the "smarts" to be afraid of defying the system. At the height of my notoriety in 2018, I often wondered if I had shot myself in the foot by coming out so publicly and aggressively. My familiar state of rebellion was so strong that I could not suppress the nurtured side of me that wanted to buck the system. However, once I discovered that the system was worth bucking, I am now trying to find out who were the people who cultivated the art of rebellion within me.

Nurtured into Innovation

If someone were to meet me today, they would see my Asian features and the way I dress for the time and my community, and they would hear my accent free voice. The assumption could be that I am American born person of Asian descent living in an American middle or upper middle-class suburb, like Silicon Valley in California or also known as the San Francisco Bay Area. The assumption would be correct. I was raised in Silicon Valley, but I am a product of the Vietnam War, once invaded by the government issued soldiers (GI's) who came in and bombed, raped, and pillaged my village, and twice by science (the(rapies).

The political climate of the time was fraught with extreme emotions in the era run by violent radical left-wing activists based out of New York City, Detroit, Chicago and Berkeley, California, inevitably going underground holding clandestine meetings to potentially overthrow the government. It has been recorded there were about 400 members of these radical left-wing activists, but I am also guessing there were many sympathizers, too. Domestic terrorism resulting in domestic casualties fueled the Federal Bureau of Investigation to keep tabs on the most influential, but it was too late, the "enemy" of the day found a way to infiltrate and find a way to seek change within its own ranks, and the path to change was through Academia.

Government issue soldiers and casualties from the war at home were not the only casualties of the war in Vietnam, but also the people of Vietnam who gave up their children witnessing and experiencing all the horrors of war. Vietnamese orphans were transported out to western countries via Operation Babylift. Subsequently upon arrival, the sickliest children were adopted by scientists equipped to handle raising children of special needs, using the babies for research, allegedly.

The height of the 1970's were one of violence, social upheaval, civil unrest, human experimentation, serial killers (Charles Manson), religious zealots, domestic terrorism, and war. Young people of the 1960's and 1970's, like my adopted parents, who were part of the Baby Boomers (1946-1964) and Silent Generations (1928-1945), fled their parents'/grandparents' PTSD and self-medicating practices such as alcoholism and abuse that were triggered by World War 1 and World War 2 which prompted them to develop a drug-using culture.

During this turbulent time of civil unrest, hippies, yippies, and yuppies turned to illicit psychedelic drugs and cannabis that were offered to them by friends and family (handlers) to cope with the extreme stress. As a result, they also opposed drafts during the Vietnam War, infusing peace and love with acts of rage and death. They were faced with either going to college or becoming a casualty to be shipped off to Southeast Asia. Not really a fine set of choices, but if a young person from the 1960's and 70's was patriotic and in fear of communism anxious to grow up, shipping off to Southeast Asia did not seem like a bad deal. However, it was not a bad deal until they saw their friends, brothers and relatives come home in caskets or the horror of lost arms, legs, and suffering from post-traumatic stress disorders. The images are hard to erase and the reactions to so much death and suffering become so extreme, there comes a tipping point, a moment of reckoning.

To make matters worse, the increased acts of police brutality against the anti-war activists and the black population stemming from years of institutionalized racism, birthed organizations like the Black Panthers and other organized leaders to strategize government overthrow. Some of the most extreme anti-war activists figured out the urban terrorism was not fruitful for their future, especially if the FBI was keeping files on the most influential. So if an anti-war or civil rights extremist like a Weather Underground member or sympathizer was to implement change, it must be done from within.

If they were to go to college to be trained in biological and intellectual modalities, there were many different breadths of study to choose from. If the students had holocaust survivors and or violence in their family backgrounds, then behavioral sciences would be appropriate to psychologically program peace and tolerance into the population. If the students had a relatively peaceful background, then the most popular, well-paid industry coupled with personality influences would lead them into chemical engineering, such as Biotechnology to genetically program people to be "peaceful". The students also studied the art of MK Ultra, which originated in the 1950s and was inspired by aggressive and militant tactics of cult brainwashing and programming of people using LSD or other drugs. The goal was probably to study how humans operate under extreme stress to squeeze out more innovation to improve society through entertainment, politics, religion, and science.

Not all scientists used strong psychedelic drugs to program their subjects. Some used behavior modification and other psychological and behavioral tactics to elicit the programming. Extreme immersion in the areas of interests along with repetition and continuous methods of negative and positive reinforcement kept sustaining the programming. Right or wrong, the scientists who saved these children from imminent death had the best of intentions, even if the process of saving these children turned out to be more than they bargained for.

With all the innovation of genetic engineering of designer babies, militant behavior modification, advanced pharmaceuticals, and holistic living in the 1980's, 1990's, and 2022+, we are currently experiencing the fallout of our parents' methods of fostering peace, love, and innovation which resulted in extreme suffering, caused by the government, or academia. As a result of compartmentalizing our parents, guardians, and government workers, how can we hold a grudge against those who applied aggressive child rearing or holistic medicine/medicine? To answer the question, I suppose we cannot hold a grudge against those of the past. I mean, civilizations always rose and fell, and there was always a catalyst, the overpopulation of humans and animals and the breakdown of the human genome.

In 2022, present day, we are experiencing explosions of cancer, disease, chronic illness, autoimmune disorders, endless cures, violence, murders, drug wars and the prevalence of oncology, oh, the irony of it all. The irony is, during this period of climate change, my protocol, the Jilly Juice LLC recipe, and protocol is not only about releasing oneself from the choice of natural/synthetic medicine but also about dealing with the war inside the body and repair the casualties from past biotechnological and the behavioral modifications.

I have literally opened my system up to take in all evolutionary intellectual and microbial information. I have no need to stop the body from the painful release as I understand why I had so much accumulation of generational intellectual and microbial information literally strangulating my ability to evolve and adapt.

Now I am proposing in 2022, those of you who feel so inclined to redirect their focus around pain and symptoms and if it is biologically feasible, to please get permission from your doctor and support system to attempt the journey. We have four generations of war to purge out and four more to teach a new and different way to deal with disease and death. I am a child of the Vietnam War that was fought externally, but I am witnessing another war that is being fought internally and the war is all around me. The suffering and death is everywhere.

With all the innovation recorded on the World Wide Web, an advanced discerning person will repair themselves and revolutionize themselves without anyone putting their hands on them. The stress and pain of becoming whole again will innovate them reminding them never to let their body, mind and spirit get so bad ever again. It is time for a rebirth.

It is time to grow another arm of the hydra.

CHAPTER 2

CLIMATE CHANGE

Climate Change Seems like War!!

ET ME HIT YOU WITH some really interesting facts. There are 5 million, trillion, trillion microbes on planet Earth made up of hydra, born from water and during its evolutionary conversion developed the Universe with diverse life. All humans have approximately 39 trillion immortal germline cells made up of diverse hydra and 30 trillion somatic cells made up of other supportive microbes acting as soldiers and specialists developing resources, and artilleries necessary to defend and ensure its own existence. Each immortal germline cell developed its own community to evolve and adapt and discard what did not work and merge in with those who can support its advancement, called symbiotes or sustaining a symbiotic relationship.

In a perfect world, diversity gets along "swimmingly", and everything is peaceful, productive, balanced, and innovative. Unfortunately, the collective life as we know it, is not in that stage of development. Life as we know it is at war with itself, each other, and is also embarking on a new stage of existence. Planet Earth, which is a microcosmic reflection of other worlds and planetary/solar systems in outer space is actively going through an aggressive evolution built for the change of climate, which has also happened before based upon evidence from antiquity, and most humans are resisting the changes, while some are realizing they must ride it out and hope they survive.

The 4ᵗʰ Turning

We are in a Great Reset which started in 9/11/2001 during the beginning of the 4th Turning[1] and the end of an 80-year cycle divided into 4 turns. Each turn lasts approximately 20+ years and those years could be war, peace, innovation, and prosperity. For example, let us take the United States of America and our war for independence. You see every 20 years major innovation and significant events happen and at the 80-year mark, a climax or a great turn of events happen. If you ever studied domestic violence, there is a term for it called

[1] https://pubmed.ncbi.nlm.nih.gov/17642125/

"the cycle of violence" and each progressive cycle of a tension building phase, the explosion or actual energetic sequence ends up in an evolutionary outcome; either someone dies or someone leaves, or a new life and innovation develops from leaving that relationship of ideas, people, places and things.

Date/War/Innovation	+80	Date/War/Innovation
1776 American War for Independence from England	+80	1856 American Civil War beginning i.e. anti-slavery and the start of the Union.
1856	+80	1936 World War II (on the heels of the 1918 Spanish Flu and World War 1) The ending of the League of Nations and development of NATO from these wars.
1936	+80	2016 The Jilly Juice (jillyjuice.com) (Life/Salt/Water/Probiotics) 2019 COVID 19 Pandemic Era mass casualties and the Exodus/Genesis of the New World going into 2096

What I have suggested sounds like a conspiracy theory, but with any theory, there are layers and layers of reasoning behind the theory. Since mankind with unfettered access to resources has proven to be too smart for his/her own good in certain circumstances, mankind can also destroy himself, when given the chance because he also strategized himself into a corner he or she cannot get out of. In order for all mankind to survive this 4th turning called climate change, mankind must be able to let go of all preconceived notions regarding politics, religion and scientific dogmas and be open to evolutionary thoughts and ideas, even if they conflict with their own.

In order to save mankind, mankind must find a way to evolve into a more adaptable, dependable, strong, and intellectual species. This line of thought also applies to the individual, not just the collective. Which means the old ways of doing things and living in homogenized and compartmentalized societies are going to the wayside, and a new innovation full of diversity is awaiting. What does this mean exactly?

Each phase of the turning involves the human species and animals harboring trillions and trillions of intelligent microbes all trying to survive and reproduce at the same time, but once the energy or hydra converts to the new model, the old model disappears, and the new model emerges. Humans and animals in the past were bred to meet specific needs, including reproduction, survival, and death, just as they are today. By the way, yes you can stay alive during this energy conversion and all energy conversion in the future (living indefinitely), but it is painful. You must also prepare your body, mind, and spirit for the next turning because it is happening, and you are seeing many people refuse to assimilate and survive the rebirthing process and those are the died suddenly people.

There is a way to counteract this situation of climate change, so it does not affect you permanently. The whole point of this book is to inform you how climate change will affect your immune system and your lifespan expectations, as well as what the system's ultimate goals are. I am not a doctor or a health professional, but I was raised by scientists, and I understand the bigger picture given how I was raised, the religions I was raised with, and all of my exposure to many politics, religion, and scientific dogmas. I do not claim the answers I have are the answers for everyone, but I do claim where science is concerned, anything is possible if you understand physics, chemistry, math, biochemistry, biology and enjoy learning and researching. The time has come to learn who and what created the systems that allow us to develop civilizations that evolve to meet the needs of each generation.

CHAPTER 3

THE ROSICRUCIAN ORDER

The Rosicrucian Order

HUMANS, YOU ARE NOT WINE, which gets better with age, you are human, who become more intelligent with maturity. An impressive sign of maturity is understanding why and how storylines become developed and to be open to hearing a different perspective. And so with that said, the "Illuminati" or the Rosicrucian Order are not only the same thing but are also called the Freemasons, which have been embedded in your community. Again, the Freemasons are the Rosicrucian Order, the Illuminati or also known as the Jewish Mystics (Sumer) (sacred geometry), Christian Gnostics (Christianity) and the Hermetics (Greco-Roman Pantheon) tracing back to at least the 17th Century. All other Eastern religions and any other philosophies recorded in ancient texts and cultures developed their own storyline versions of those who came before them. My focus from here on out is more from a Western perspective, not discounting those not mentioned, but the West needs to understand who they are, and where they came from and why such a mixture in diversity. Let us explore the alchemy of the illuminated Rosicrucian Freemason Society and their imprint on humanity throughout the ages of the world.

During periods of technological and scientific advancements, past and present civilizations rise or fall based on how much pressure builds up within a society and then when the pressure finally releases. While the technological advancements may change within each period of advancement, the edification of new societies picking up where their ancestors left off, still must follow a uniform development of systems of rise, and then a controlled system decline. Since advanced societies communicate through languages and frequencies through allegories offered by politics, religions, and science, the process of reproducing the same system with different "products" or ideas will also undergo numerous name changes hence why there are different names for the same thing. Different names for the same type of persons, places, things, or ideas is strategy to reinvent the wheel, but make the wheel better with a different outcome. Reinventing "new" and "better" or more advanced humans reflective of their advanced society is exactly what we are embarking on right now during this great reset.

All Humans have untapped potential, ancient knowledge deep within their immune systems because they hold DNA from past civilizations from their ancestors who underwent many years of trauma and innovation to move humanity forward. Many humans will never know the potential they hold within, because they were programmed to live and die once their strongest resources were exploited. On the other hand, many humans will discover how valuable they are to themselves in their world and will realize, it is time to uncork the bottle (their immune system) and relieve the pressure and let the gifts of humanity pour out without destroying others.

The United States of America is just that example of how much innovation is held within our DNA given we are a melting pot of innovation and cultures from all over the world. Not only have we underwent sociopolitical experiments and change, but we have been undergoing biological experimental change developing into streamlines of communication and information. However, during the process of experimentation leading to innovation evolution, the methods used are also emotionally dark and messy with periodic moments of awareness and light.

The Hydra or Eye of Ra in Poli(ticks), Relig(ion)and Sc(i)ence

The Eye of Ra or hydra represents the one eyed single celled organism; the basis of all life forms, which mutate and evolve that are also in all the symbols those in the conspiracy world dubbed Illuminati Symbols. The hand over one eye, the one-eyed jack, the all-seeing eye, and cartoon characters with one eye all represent the power of hydra or life and the evolution of life using proteins to develop diverse versions of itself. Scientific explorers hunt for more diverse hydra to develop a more advanced human and animal and plant species is an ongoing thing and celebrated in small circles, especially in the science community.

Those who do not understand science and how to control their own microbes, will have an issue with bringing more evolution to a diverse population because they are barely surviving the diversity they have in their own body, their community and even in their family. The phonetics of the word tick in politics, and ion in the word religion is the worshipping of energy since ion is energy found in the ionosphere and salt and water. Science phonetically sounds like eye, or someone sighing, around the eye, the study of the one-eyed organism intelligent enough to evolve and become advanced.

The all-seeing eye on top of the capstone on a pyramid, found on the dollar bill, represents the Holy Trinity, the stability of the proteins based upon the intelligence of the hydra's ability to evolve and put communities together to keep reinventing itself by converting its own proteins to become adaptable to its own environment. All religions are based upon stable proteins and unstable proteins and science studies them, and politics allocates energy to support and study the infrastructure needed to evolve and ensure its own survivability.

Based on the Rosicrucian Order, which combines Jewish Mysticism, Christian Gnosticism, and Hermeticism, Western Civilization has symbols representing a balance between life and death. Numerology or the study of the meaning of numbers based upon chemistry and allegory also have their own distinct patterns of influence between limbo or crossroads, life, and death. No matter whether you subscribe to an organized thought process or not, politics, religion, and science are all fused into these symbols.

Judaism/Jewish Mysticism/6 Points/Star of David	Christianity/Christian Gnosticism/4 Points/Cross	Satanism/Hermeticism/5 Points/Pentagram
Stability: Two triangles and 1 inverted (made up of 3 points each) All stable proteins have three folds to them. [1] To balance out life, death must also occur at the micro-level and macro-level	Crossroad: 1 Cross meaning the Christians are at a crossroad/choice between two options: Balancing Life/Death with the Star of David or Satanism (Hermeticism (medicine) also known as instability with the Pentagram Upside down cross meaning a healing crisis vs an upside right cross "cured" until a healing crisis and this is where the rubber meets the road.	Death/Evolution: Instability or when one triangle/protein is misfolded causing anomalies in the DNA and RNA, called autophagy with an occasional apoptosis Worshipping death and evolution is a religion and it is everywhere. Is it really death or just another form of life? Is it one form of life converting into another form of life? Is the old form of life compatible with the new form life?

Scientifically speaking, the above illustrates how stable proteins structures are [2] held together by chains of amino acids linked together by peptide bonds representing life. Unstable proteins also called denaturization when the sequence of unfolding causes the weakest elemental makeup of the protein to break apart relative to the small positive/negative interactions. In other words, this mechanism represent autophagy, which I will cover in later chapters.

When you think about the symbols above, The Trinity, or Catholicism is the best way to explain what is going on right now. Before I came to this conclusion about humans and religion, I had to study all the players of antiquity and even the Middle Ages to understand what icons of the past represented. I figured out that Jesus Christ represents all of mankind at the crossroads of their evolution. They can either turn to Judaism, or the Star of David and become a stable protein folded in thirds and live on and adapt, or they turn to

---

[2] https://www.nature.com/scitable/topicpage/protein-structure-14122136/?fbclid=IwAR0x-Yauz4MH-CNjDpXpxQgswPFnd0CRBMs-MAVwR70tsgBcZ-MbLV9ZW4Q

instability, the darkness and become a ghost or die becoming part of the netherworld. In essence, the Father the Son and the Holy Ghost explain just that. The Father is you/Jesus, and the Son/Sun is light, Lucifer (bringer of light), who also kills, and the Holy Ghost or Satan, the Prince of Darkness, who also kills. How can the Sun/Son or Lucifer kill? Because too much light/life can destroy a person, called irradiation, and so the darkness controls the light, and the light controls the darkness, and both must be balanced. In other words, mushrooms grow in darkness while weed or marijuana must grow in the light. When it is all said and done, aging is irradiation on the inside or too much life on the inside of the person causing rapid growth, early sexuality, and early disease and premature death.

The Georgia Guidestones

The Georgia Guidestones, I speculate, were developed by the order as the tablet for change like the 10 Commandments in the 5 Books of Moses. It is a light or dark depiction of evolution and transition from the old world to the new world. Since I lightly studied change management with various adult education classes, the tenets of the Georgia Guidestones are not unlike mission statements in organizations with a purpose. Humans have a purpose, and their purpose changes daily, weekly, monthly, and even every 100 years, at the turn of the century, or otherwise known as The Turning. The Georgia Guidestones like the 10 Commandments below have a common theme of controlling fertility, national sovereignty, balance, natural law, and tolerance to diversity.

How can one possibly argue with this notion? Well, honestly, if one chooses not to assimilate to the climate change, regardless of what catalyzed the change, it is safe to assume they have made a conscious choice to resist. Theoretically, resistance is futile, especially since we cannot control everything in this world. When I finally stopped resisting things I seriously could not control, so many awakenings were right at my fingertips speaking to me in my dreams manifesting into ideas, words and thought processes.

Georgia Guidestones

1. *Maintain humanity under 500,000,000 in perpetual balance with nature.*

2. *Guide reproduction wisely—improving fitness and diversity.*

3. *Unite humanity with a living new language.*

4. *Rule passion—faith—tradition—and all things with tempered reason.*

5. *Protect people and nations with fair laws and just courts.*

6. *Let all nations rule internally, resolving external disputes in a world court.*

7. *Avoid petty laws and useless officials.*

8. *Balance personal rights with social duties.*

9. *Prize truth—beauty—love—seeking harmony with the infinite.*

10. *Be not a cancer on the Earth—Leave room for nature— Leave room for nature.*

Jillian, are you saying they are doing population control on purpose? All I can prove is we, as a society have been warned about climate change in all the politics, and if you have been to college, studying organizational development or business process reengineering, you had the choice to choose those classes as a major and minor to implement and support climate change. Biotechnology, information technology and best practices are all lucrative fields to study in, so that should have been some kind of indicator. Is anything organic? In my opinion, no it is not. Energy cannot be created or destroyed, only converted. If you want to bring something back to life, it must have an organized infrastructure to support that life. If you want to convert life or evolve life, you must have the climate and environmental conditions to support that transition along with a sound infrastructure.

Now that I know life can be converted into so many different possibilities, all the changes going on are exactly what humanity has gone through before until humanity finally gets it right. No different than a human continuously dying and reproducing until that spirit of that human finally gets it right. It is like a spiritual falling down, and then getting up and trying again, over, and over and over again. No matter what life forms it takes on, it will always transform and manifest in the appropriate dimension, like the paranormal, appropriate to the choices and experiences it underwent in its previous life form.

The Paranormal

Anyone who has watched celebrities on television has probably seen some type of ghost paranormal show exploiting the celebrity's ability to communicate with the dead. Personally, I was not into the paranormal so much during my late 20s and 30s, except playing with a Ouija Board when I was in my late teens, and early 20s. Of course, I was naïve to the power of parasitic influential entities finding their way into my soul and attaching themselves to me, but it was a world that fascinated me until I was so scared from a "sign", that I got rid of the board extremely fast. I mean, this was in the early 1990s and I just turned 19 and so once I conjured up something a little weird, I decided that playing in the spirit world was not for me, or so I thought.

Fast forward to 2010, my interest in the paranormal world was reignited by my soon to be husband in Ohio, after I trekked across the USA in search of a better life. All the ghost shows he introduced to me were about spotting orbs of energy that were floating around intelligently in high electrical environments that experienced tremendous amounts of energy at the time of their existence. Some of the infrared cameras that even the energy look so organized it would project sticklike images on the screen. The voice boxes used to capture the energy and intelligence of the spirit has also been a source of fascination, kind of.

During this climate change of 2022 and the COVID-19 era of disease, I have also witnessed orblike entities on my computer screen and even felt a presence in my room as I was coughing out the hydra that was once stuck in my colon, but my immune system finally pushed it out.

I also realize that fertilization happens in both the dead world and the waking world and when you are sleeping, it is like you are "dead" to the world at the time of your slumber. Fertilizing an egg with sperm happens in the waking world developing life and you wake up from a sleep, or a child is conceived. Fertilizing someone to die is during the night is when the body is deciding if it has enough life to carry it through and wake up in the morning.

Once the body finds out it does not have enough life in it to fight against the "demons", the body goes through, yet another energetic conception called cardiac arrest or sudden death from the energetic event attempting to live and is fertilized into the microbial world otherwise known as the "afterlife". The only way people survive events like these is if they are aware they must change and support all events like these as they become less aggressive. If a person is not aware enough to change for the better to support being fertilized into the next waking life on Earth via Evolution, then they get fertilized into the paranormal or death and hope they can assimilate to another human host in the waking world and become part of a collective allowed to live, yet again, essentially starting over again.

Since fertility can go one of two ways, life, and death, all the stories, allegories from television shows, books, magazines, movies, religious texts, star seed new age beliefs, horoscopes, politics, religions, and all scientific dogmas all support both fertilizing people into life and death at their own hand.

The Rosicrucian Order is giving everyone a choice to become part of the New World Order or resist themselves out of existence. Instead of mankind being the one to determine who lives and who dies, mankind is leaving it up to the microbial world and the climate change and force people to either fertilize themselves into death or life through their inability or ability to adapt to the changing biological, geopolitical, climate and economic changes. If a person is unaware of their choices, they become part of the walking dead, or those who are in limbo between life and death, it will take just one energetic event to zap them into the next level of evolution via particle acceleration.

Particle (seed) Acceleration

In conclusion to all the above, Pandora's Box has been opened, and you cannot stuff the Genie back in the bottle because everything that is happening was meant to happen. When I was staring at my sliding glass door and the hot afternoon sun was shining through the slats blinding me, I was looking at so many particles or dust particles, microbial particles, virus particles, bacteria particles, or HYDRA particles. When I zoomed in on the plasma reflecting in the sun beams, the orblike energies were extremely diverse. Then I realized, if I were to blow a fan with non-toxic refrigerants and or blow a fan with non-toxic heat, the particle accelerators change the climate in my house to make it warm or cold, relative to my comfort level. If it is "dusty" in my house, I could sneeze or get sick if I had issues with some of the microbes floating around. Long story short, climate change is HVAC (heating ventilation and air conditioning), which is particle acceleration using high frequency transmitters and is a weather particle accelerator in your home to influence climate control and cool or heat up areas needing temperature, cosmetic or structural changes.

As we live in such a vast universe, we have no idea where all the original catalysts for weather, wind, rain, and seasonal changes came from. As a result, climate change may have been intentionally conceived with the intent of realizing the Georgia Guidestones. However, it may have evolved organically into the Georgia Guidestones as a result of the notion that climate change will inevitably happen at some point. Mainstream thought processes and conspiracy theorists alike will forever speculate about it.

By accelerating particles in response to or in relation to this 4th turning of evolution, humans will be introducing so much diversity, chaos, and change into the world, forcing everyone to reassess what it means to live as a human controlling their own biodiversity in their body, mind, and spirit, justifying their beliefs through politics, religions, and all science dogmas. As humans, we will literally seed ourselves into life or the afterlife.

But wait… there is a catch… to survive what might be a "proverbial purge". You must know the difference between an open system and a closed system and how autophagy (cell breakdown) and fertility (cell reproduction) and high frequency and low frequency all work together. You will explore those pairs in the next chapter, "Diversity".

The Rosicrucian Order is Giving You A Choice

CHAPTER 4

DIVERSITY: INTRODUCING AN OPEN SYSTEM

THE TERM DIVERSITY HAS BEEN personally hijacked by so many different special interest groups who claim one thing or another, but in all reality, diversity is about redefining what was defined in one system and developing a different definition in another system. I am not saying people did not have a good reason for claiming diversity representing their lifestyle and belief system, but if one group or many groups claim diversity is tolerance, then we must be tolerant to all lifestyles and belief systems so as long as they follow the lines of the law. Diversity does not discriminate because diversity implies the acceptance of an open system working alongside closed systems.

With that said, with this climate change going on, thermodynamically open and closed systems are one of many options to choose once the whole world understands the benefits and drawbacks of both lifestyles. If it is assumed that all societies have worked from thermodynamically closed systems, and I would say that is a safe assumption, then presenting an argument for a thermodynamically open system is completely appropriate. To make it even easier to grasp, the word ecosystem is a good jumping off point to exemplify how thermodynamically open and closed ecosystems determine peace, war, calm and conflict.

For example, both the internal ecosystem and external ecosystem in all plants, animals and insects are run by the microbial world such as the hydra and tardigrades which evolved from the hydra, and they must have all types of water to survive. Of course there are hydra composites of microbial species that by themselves are unique, but when they collectively align they may also be a creature of extraordinary capabilities.

The hydra have a "closed" system, which means one opening (one eye) takes in food and releases waste and mainly survives in temperate climates and are the intelligence of all life in space and on Earth. On the other hand, the tardigrades, another microbial 8-legged specie, known as "the slow stepper", derived from the hydra have been found in space and Earth in all sorts of climates have an open system, with food going in one opening and waste coming out the other end.

Over trillions of years the evolution of the hydra developing into an adaptable tardigrade along with all the 5million trillion trillion microbes all over planet Earth, of course intelligent life such as **_humans_** emerged. With humans made up of 39 trillion hydra immortal germline microbes and 30 trillion hydra protein cells making up its own infrastructure, mankind has been able to build himself a nice community with creature comforts. Creature is the proverbial word.

Since water is the basis of life made up of hydra and hydra floating in your plasma air such as in your home and outside, humans, animals and plants will always be exposed to simple and advanced forms of hydra floating in their air, water, and body which has a huge percentage of plasma or water and are full of hydra microbes. More importantly, hydra are so energetic, mineralizing the public water supply became necessary because the people drinking the untreated water were deteriorating from all the hydra life forms.

Humans, made up of 69 trillion hydra are extremely intelligent and has figured out how to asexually reproduce or sexually reproduce which is based upon how advanced it has become. The life forms that evolved from the hydra, developed indicators or messaging systems to instruct their colonies to either; encourage autophagy-breaking down, and fertility-building up or breaking down and building up simultaneously called: senescence-autophagy, evolution-autophagy-fertility, entropy-autophagy, or fertility-building up-autophagy triggering fertility, infection, fetus, sepsis, cancer, disease, and chronic illness. It might seem rather confusing, but I will not fall into the rabbit holes of compartmentalizing fertility and autophagy, especially when it comes to hydra. You see hydra are the basis of thermodynamics and hydra cannot be created or destroyed, only converted. Autophagy, fertility and all the words attached to those two specific words mean hydra/energy can never be destroyed. In essence, death means the person or animal goes back to square one, a single celled amoeba, dying to be part of another community. Life is just life. Death is also a conversion process reducing a colony down to its most common denominator, the single hydra. Now you might see where I am going here.

For the life of me, trying to figure out how to explain the constant action/reaction/action reaction of substance added and substance taken away based upon intention is like herding kittens. No matter how I try to break down entropy (breaking down) and negentropy (combining), which are loosely based on the 3 Laws of Thermodynamics, they are all based on hydra and their offspring, which are all the microbes that evolved into the animal kingdom. In this world of intention, internal frequencies, and external frequencies, it is impossible to create an "absolute chart" or graph to depict how life governs itself.

Check out the concentric circles below and relative to each other they are either internal or external relative to your perspective of inside one circle outside another circle. Each circle has its own frequency from the center point all the way out to the hinterlands. If one wanted to develop diverse civilizations with diverse or homogenized life forms, each concentric circle would be governed by its own frequency, infrastructure, lifestyle, belief systems and purpose.

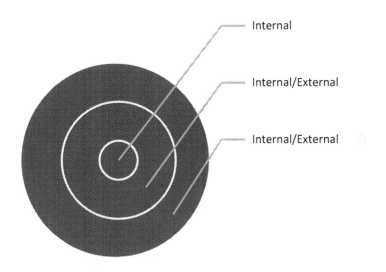

Now take the same notion to a human, and realize each human is holding their own unique internal frequencies subjected to the external frequencies and every reaction to the external frequencies are different but the same. Pretend the circles are diverse individual human bodies in homogenized environments of universal frequencies, but each homogenized environment may also have their different frequencies in the environment based upon internal influences. Now picture the frequencies of humans to be their blood types of ABO and the RH factor and now another layer of frequencies need to be considered when dealing with diversity, climate change and undefined life and defined death. Now, can you see the layers and layers of considerations when understanding lifestyles, belief systems, body types and their tolerance for autophagy/ fertility pain and diversity?

In regard to a person's immune system, relative to their blood type, the constant antigen-antibody reactions determine how much energy that person is carrying and supporting which also contribute to lifespans relative to an open system or a closed system. The frequent hydra energy of the antigen-antibody programming can be extremely influential in either an open or closed system, and so it is important to understand why it is not just about frequencies, it is about how high frequencies and low frequencies develop into conflict when not managed carefully.

Conflicting Frequencies

Developing frequency "binary" driven arguments of morals and judgements based on perception of what is good or what is bad has steered humanity into accepting death as life and life as death with no in between. The fact humans have mischaracterized symptom frequencies of pain and developed campaigns both for and against arguments around "suffering" to save one's life also has caused such confusion and the notion that suffering is bad across the board had caused people to be cured and die as soon as the climate changes.

Diversity is all about understanding the power of suffering through symptoms and feeding symptoms of new life and releasing the "old life" and still keep the parent cells or humans intact and still alive. I remember someone saying, watch for the Saviors in your community. They will save you to death and then say they saved you. So when they prescribe to you prostaglandin inhibitors, and you get relief from the painful release, but die from too much fertility during the climate change, this is how saviors save people to death.

When medication, anti-inflammatories, surgeries, herbs, remedies and all the aggressive spices are used to stop the prostaglandins from pushing out the old world through diarrhea, sweat, mucus, poop, and pee, and not allowing the new world of evolution to take hold, the animal, entity, and human become cannibalized by the diverse number of generations trapped in the body regardless of size. Over time, a war is developed between all the diverse hydra trapped in a closed system and then mutually assured destruction is inevitable. It is like housing the Baby Boomers, Gen X, Gen Y, Gen Alpha, Gen Beta, and they all are fighting each other to the death to be the one in control. The parent or the host trying to manage all the diversity within its world then becomes cannibalized by the energy because the system all the diversity lives within is a closed system.

More importantly, diverse sexual orientation also comes out of closed systems because the diversity are trapped with each other with no other choices but to keep reproducing behaviors, phenotypical characteristics and genotypical characteristics. If any part of the host is traumatized, their hydra exhibit anomalous behaviors that then shape the life of the host forever unless the host releases the hydra by conditioning the body to release the traumatized hydra and take on new information, essentially new memories.

The core issue today, people are not releasing the trauma of their injured hydra memories and so radicalism, extremism and intolerance are the common ground, for now, and it is taking society down actively accelerated by climate change, the heating up of the planet. If one wants to survive climate change, they must open up their system.

An open system, at some point, under the control of their doctor, stops taking medication to constrict the prostaglandins from releasing the offspring of hydra torturing them with disease. These hydra offspring are developed daily, hourly, and minutely, when a host enters into different microbiomes like crowded places or even outside on a windy rainy day. By releasing offending colonies of hydra that threaten the host, a hydra encourages an open system, much like calling the police or chasing away a robber. Once the host colony has assimilated to the new information/hydra it has encountered, it will mature the new guests, so there will be no spread of disease.

When the body or host is triggered to encourage a release to push out offending colony forming units of hydra, the host will use food and cough, sneeze, blow the nose, poop, and sweat to take the place of hormone replacement therapy, pills, powders, supplements, remedies, and surgeries. ***_Then, the host will be the best prototype, with no desire to have a child, much less experience a disease, and live an undefined, indefinite life._***

However, that may seem easier said than done. Since we have been brought up in a closed system with diverse sexual orientations and all kinds of exotic diseases, Mother Earth needs to recalibrate and start her engines up and change up all the climates, so the fertility of diseases and the autophagic release of proteins are so exponential, people and animals who are not conditioned to climate change and high frequency environments die suddenly or contract a disease. If people fed all their disease food and released their demons, so to speak, and blew their nose, coughed, sneezed, pooped, peed, and sweat, they could potentially survive climate change.

What humans must be aware of as they are shifting to a more open system, if possible, their phenotypical characteristics will change through the transition and people will not look "cured" or like their prior programming. They will look either extremely skinny or extremely obese or "normal" holding the line of acceptable aesthetics. The issue is those who are cured or closed, may not survive climate change and those who sustain their intention to open their system have a better chance.

I must remember that no matter what someone looks like, acts like, or sounds like, I cannot assume anything about their lifestyle and belief system around life, longevity and health and wellness. That goes for animals, too. Many people's animals and children and themselves will be going through a metamorphosis and there is no way to know if the animal will survive or not survive the climate change regardless of their beliefs in the medical/holistic system.

Of course, I can speculate who will survive and who will not, but at this point, when people are dependent on the health and wellness industry, there is no guarantee with anything because the medical system practices medicine and innovates people through suffering like surgeries, and also takes away their suffering, ultimately ending up in rest in peace. Of course using the medical and holistic system is one choice of a closed system, but there is another choice, an open system and the medical and holistic system might need to change to accommodate another option.

There is no such thing as "immortality" in the broader sense because a large asteroid can deplete a large area. It is recognizing undefined lives means indefinite life because life is not defined by a lifespan, but by how they support the life in their body and if they support an open system or a closed system. Conditioning oneself internally by balanced release and balanced retention through salt, water, food, air, rest, and movement will help any host of a diverse hydra microbiome survive any sort of climate change.

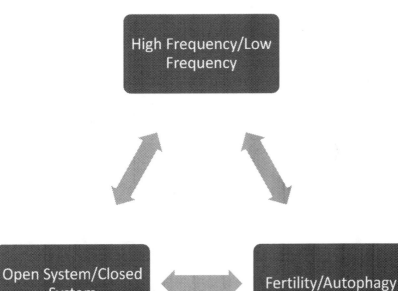

THE NEXT CHAPTER

THE JILLY JUICE JOURNEY CONVERSION PROCESS

WELL... THE JOURNEY OF THIS conversion process of this book is nearing an end. It has been such a wild ride getting to this point of physical and mental clarity. It has taken 3 books in 6 years and thousands of voices in opposition and also support, to learn how the world works. This section merely gives you a glimpse of how I was able to convert to be an open system from being a closed system. I am not even mentioning blood types as a "target type to be" because blood types are irrelevant when my system is either open or closed. A person's blood type is only necessary when they are closed, as the medical system must establish conditional therapy that distinguishes blood types. In emergency situations, universal blood types donate their blood so anyone can use it regardless of blood types. Other than conditional therapies, blood types are just programming that will be released, and new hydra and microbial programming is gained. Will that new programming be gained so much it causes a new blood type? Only in a closed system. An open system I will take advantage of all microbial programming available to me. However, in order to receive that luxury, I must suffer, at my own accord, to release the old -world programming, which I did, and take on the new world programming.

No way, in any shape or form am I recommending Jilly Juice and the suffering that goes along with it to anyone, whether on their own or with a doctor, and I am not saying just anyone can do it. That is not for me to determine who should suffer the pain of disease and who should not. No one but a licensed professional cause someone's suffering or take away someone's suffering/rest in peace. Many people have admonished me in the media saying I should only be getting recommendations from a doctor to end my own suffering in climate change. In essence, what they are implying is I destroy myself with medicines to stop the release of energy and die. Of course that is not what they meant, however, doctors practice medicine and so do veterinarians. If people are assuming the medicine for myself and my animal will work the same way it did 20 years ago or even 2 years ago, they could be sorely mistaken. The frequencies and climate change stipulate efficacy of all medications and the medications during this climate change could have the opposite intention, even more suffering or a died suddenly situation. With that said, all my accounts given below regarding my own journey in the JJ world and how I characterize energy is just another arm of the hydra. Of course everything I am saying is subject to my opinion, my belief, and my truth and is in no way saying my truth is any better than your truth.

In my opinion, it is high time we know why pain happens and why people recommend stopping it and why the medical and holistic industry were developed with so many professionals and lay people with their multi-level-marketing gigs selling us a remedy or a pill. Since I am willing to face the pain of suffering of releasing my own demons and building myself up, I choose to share my journey, even if it conflicts with everyone.

Just to be clear, in no way am I giving anyone medical

advice and there is no such thing as "normal". There is such thing as change, evolution, internal frequency of antigen-antibody programming (conflicting hydra developing offspring of life), and external frequency of the climate or environment. The JJ Journey is a slow salt and water conditioning process of the energetic release of the microbial hydra babies meant to be released. The reason why they were not released was because the person mischaracterized the energy and ingested medicine to stop the suffering of releasing the demons, called prostaglandin inhibitors, thus trapping the diverse babies inside. Instead of just learning how to blow one's nose, cough extremely deeply and find ways to digitally understand their alimentary canal, people tend to gravitate towards the medicines to stop their body from releasing.

In turn, over many years of anti-inflammatory practices, the microbes built up exponentially that even daily bathroom habits are not enough, and diarrhea is "out of the question", and so all those microbes which turn into massive colony forming units become too much for people to manage hence the reason why the medical and holistic system promotes so many different therapies such as extreme diets and exercise regimes and even surgeries. In the past, the starvation of my microbes only made them extremely mad, and they turned on me, eating up the infrastructure of my body, hence why some people develop open sores of infection or experience system deterioration.

If a person in the diet world has not conditioned themselves to eat all the food, because of some prior fear of genetically modified, meat, milk, eggs, fruits and veggies, nuts, and oils, then the weaning off the diets and ingesting all food must be a gradual process. The whole point is to replenish their fatty acids, amino acids, prohormones, and minerals with all the foods they were ever afraid of. Of course, if a person is not strong enough, they must ask their doctor for assistance. In other words the gradual food intake is based upon the body's needs at the time, especially in a higher frequency environment like storms and season changes.

When the environment is highly dynamic, the energy or hydra in my plasma are also highly frenetic, hence the feelings of the body pushing out unwanted organisms called pain. Even more importantly, any time mucus forms from food or air and water exposure, it is all life. The fact mucus developed meant life was able to grow inside the body and the waste was able to leave the body, which is why mucus can work for me or against me. If mucus wants to leave, I blow my nose, diarrhea and sweat. It is when people stuff the mucus back in the body with aggressive topical and internal agents that over time, work against the person causing massive amounts of growth and in different environments, too much mass works against the person. Not enough mass does not allow the body to build up blood pressure to carry nutrients and oxygen to the heart.

All in all, the individual must be savvy enough to know how to listen to their body's indicators of hunger, fatigue, bloating and pain. The antigen-antibody programming causing so much pain usually resides in the gut or lower intestines and there are ways to dig out the software in the body and release the "demons" providing relative relief.

I figured out the way to release my own demons during the worst times of being sick the last two years and it was a 6-year conditioning process, starting in 2016. Most people are not comfortable with digitally digging out the old software programming, so they see their doctor, but humans were meant to be self-sufficient and undeterred by their own bodily fluids and body parts. The fact we have scared ourselves away from self-sufficiency says a whole lot about how much money is in managed health care.

On that note of tolerance, I have also learned not to use the word obese or emaciated because the terms are pejorative, and size is relative to the state of their internal ecosystem and external environment and what it takes for them to survive. Salt and water condition the vital organs to deal with a higher frequency environment, and of course a higher sodium intake with salting in food will allow the body to develop mass and substance and insulation. The annual saltwater flushes I employed for my regiment were the retroactive release of the metastasizing offspring colonizing so many different parts of the body. And so I had to feel energy/pain of release if I wanted to prolong my life. In this environment, I will not need as many saltwater flushes because the energy in the environment has already woken up the beasts within. Now I must feed all energy with all food and feel the release and find ways to pull out the colonies of hydra in my colon residing in my poop.

It is not glamourous and if it is too difficult, people always asked their physician what they could do to help move their bowels. I discovered that salt and water and milk are great initial catalysts to help me move the colonies out of my gut, and I still drink milk today, but like anything if I had any allergies and issues, I would have had to talk to my doctor.

The graph below is a hypothetical composite of how most people operate when it comes to their thermodynamically open or closed alimentary canal, like hydra in the tardigrade, which are the most effective organized efficient digestive system. From my vantage point, all four lifestyles based upon how the human reacts to and manages their energy are all fine. If one wanted to redirect to open and then closed, or closed then open, they have the chance, providing they understand what it takes on both ends. It is easy to be closed and feel no pain or symptoms of release, but if a person stays too closed, people tend to stay closed until they pass away.

Opening oneself up may prove too painful, which therein lies the issue. The suffering of deterioration is what the medical/holistic system tries to temper, but at some point, there is nothing the medical or holistic system can do. If I can drop seeds to those who are in the position to convert from a closed system to an open system, that is literally my goal in life. I know not everyone can, and I am sorry. I wish I had this information sooner, but even if I had the information sooner, would people still consider the possibility?

The Alimentary Canal (Tardigrade)~ Undefined

Life = ∞, until I redirect the motion

	Open/(No Diets) Closed/ (Cured) *Chance to Redirect* It is painful.	Closed (Diets) Closed (Cured) *Chance to Redirect* It is painful.	Closed (Diets) Open (Not Cured) *Chance to Redirect* It is painful.	**Open (No Diets) Open (Not Cured) Undefined Life** Once I achieve this, it is hard to degrade.
Mouth ("open") Anus ("closed")	∞			
Mouth ("closed") Anus ("closed")		∞		
Mouth ("closed") Anus ("open")			∞	
Mouth ("open") Anus ("open")				∞

My Conversion Process The Last Six Years of My Life

In the beginning of the Jilly Juice Journey (2016), I was not prepared to get as sick as I did ever since the pandemic of 2019 happened. I was more worried about getting some type of relief from my aggressive premenstrual symptoms rearing its ugly head once a month. Having discovered how powerful salt and water with probiotics were (tested in a lab), I achieved a little peace and respite in my biological issues at the same time as dealing with lower-level symptoms at the surface, but I still had to deal with everyone questioning my reasoning that sickness would lead to healing. It was not until about 3 years later in late 2019, as I was on and off Jilly Juice, that I experienced some aggressive symptoms coming to surface I was not aware of or knew what exactly it was. What is "it"?

I had an aggressive mycoplasma mucus web of an entity living inside of me, rivaling the "blob" found in horror movies that took over people asphyxiating them or covering them from head to foot in a weblike structure. However, before I discovered that is what I was actually dealing with, ever since 2019 I experienced hive, rashes, headaches, body aches, muscle aches, respiratory infection after infection. I would be so tired at different times of the day, and I would be gaining, losing weight, and feeling bloated and irritable. My menses would be all over the place never on "schedule" like it used to be. Below was the process I had to deal with for such a long time.

My Process of Releasing the "Demons".

1. I finally stopped drinking Jilly Juice and any saltwater purges, except annually.
2. Experience Infection (symptoms) (cough, poop, blow my nose)
3. Gained weight
4. I ate all food/drank tons of milk
5. I pulled out the stagnated poop
6. I had to get sick with ALL SYMPTOMS
7. I finally lost some excess weight

Morning Routines

1. Get up and use the restroom/shower and cough and blow my nose and find ways to explore my sphincter and get the pasty/pebbly and dry poop out.

2. Hock up loogies and spit and blow my nose in the shower as hard as I can to push out the waste material on each end of my alimentary canal.

3. I had to train my body to expel mucus using muscle/mucus training my insides so when my body activates from a food or antigen/pathogen exposure, it can release those pathogens with ease.

This had to happen over and over again for the last 6 years ever since 2016, and then the climate changed in July of 2022 when I felt the frequencies of climate change trigger the ultimate infection. I essentially, systematically purged out the demons within me until I could go into a crowd of people maskless without mucusing up so much and developing an infection. This process was imperative until I purged out the demons in my whole body/immune system and I revisited old childhood issues all the way up to current issues.

I suffered ridicule from my online trolls who said I looked "unhealthy", fat, and gross. If you were wrestling with antigen-antibody demons within you, you would look like a "monster", too, and some people do when their monsters get out of control. The traditional ways of keeping the monsters within my control are temporary, and they are a short-term solution to an extremely long-term problem. The process I am going through and had went through is a long-term solution to a short-term problem in the long run. The potential for "indefinite" life is raising my expectations I have the time to redevelop the programming, so I do not die from preventable diseases, like the aging process or sudden death events.

With that said, I had to gain weight in the JJ world, and I also had to understand how to pull out the software/ feces poop that was stuck way up in my colon. I also had to really blow my nose so hard, even popping blood vessels.

Coughing was extremely necessary to push out the poop and the mucus out of my sinuses while also eating all food and retaining substance to allow for the release process. I figured out gaining weight meant that my body was preparing for the conversion process: I had to have enough substance on my body enough to carry me through converting from the old world to the new world when I suffered that coinfection of pneumonia and whatever else I had.

I also realized I had to gain so much weight the last few years because it was preparing me for the crazy coinfection I dealt with last summer of 2022 that was so intense. I did not eat hardly at all. I could barely drink water. I could barely get up and move around. I did not poop for a few days, and I just laid in bed sleeping and the body was converting itself during that time, purging out the antigen-antibody programming. If I had NOT gained weight, I would have died from a heart attack or stroke or any other predisposed issue. I could NOT get away with being as skinny as I was a few years ago in 2018 when all I did was drink my Jilly Juice, barely ate and was always on the go. The fact I knew my alimentary canal like the back of my hand, the fact I can sit with the pain of gaining weight and not looking "sexy" lol, gave my body the opportunity to store nutrients, water, and fat to carry me through the conversion process that many people have not experienced yet and are too afraid to experience the energy of coming back to life.

Metaphorically speaking, gaining weight is correlative to building up an infrastructure to support the conversion process. When the bodies/societies must purge out the excess entities/or conflicting programming, it must gain weight/ build infrastructure to support the purge process, properly. Remember, I gained weight relative to what my body needed during each environmental change in the atmosphere.

Below is the Jilly Juice Recipe, but I can now just do annual saltwater flushes because Jilly Juice is really like a saltwater recipe with probiotic friendly gut bacteria in it. The fact life was able to grow in it and it grew in an anaerobic environment with 13m colony forming units was proof it was and is not harmful, but the answer is not in the juice, it really is my level of awareness around the power of suffering through releasing the old world so I can survive this new world.

The Jilly Juice Recipe

The 3 Day Ferment and the 24-Hour Ferment:

The 3 Day Ferment:

Ingredients:

1. 1 Cups loosely packed chopped Cabbage (red or green) and/or Kale.
2. 2 Cups of Tap Water
3. 1 Tablespoon of Table Salt

Directions:

1. Place the cabbage/kale, water, and Salt together in a blender and puree. The finer the cabbage in the ferment, the easier it will be to drink.

2. Pour the mixture into my jar. The jar should appear 25% solids and 75% liquid after it settles. Until I become familiar with how much cabbage/kale needs to be used, it is best to let it settle a bit to judge the ratios, as I can adjust the ratio at this stage by adding either more pureed cabbage, or more brine (water & Salt), though there is no need for this to be a perfect ratio, it will be drinkable either way, and I can just improve this with the next batch.

3. Cover the jar with an airtight lid. (If there is exposed metal in my lid, I may use a coffee filter placed between the jar and the lid in case the lids rust and are harder to open.) Glass jars with self-locking mechanisms and rubber grommets do not need coffee filters.

4. Let mixture stand at room temperature (ferment) for at least 3 days or more until consumed or store it in refrigerator (around 65-72 degrees F). If I am in a colder climate, (less than 65 degrees in the house) leave it out longer prior to putting it in the

refrigerator. If I am in a hot climate (10 degrees or more above the recommended temperature), I can leave it out or store it in the refrigerator sooner if I like it cold. Keep the jars away from heat and flame and hot surfaces. I can shake, mix, stir or open the ferments at any time after the initial 3 days, however, it does not require burping.

5. After 3 days (72 hours) or more has passed, the fermenting is completed. Gently stir the mixture and drink (or refrigerate for later use).

6. If I am storing my ferment in the refrigerator, it is recommended to stir it or turn it upside down, if I want to check for air leaks, every day or every few days, to keep any floating solids on the top saturated with the brine. This recipe can be stored forever.

The 24-Hour Ferment (subsequent batches):

This is the same as the 3 Day Ferment, except I am using my previous ferment as a "starter" so it will only need to ferment for 24 hours, since batches using "starter" (previously completed ferments) will be finished much faster.

Directions: Use a small portion of the last ferment as a starter to decrease the time necessary for the batch to ferment.

Approximately 1/4 - 1/2 Cup of previously made 3 Day Ferment per batch. (If I am using a gallon sized jar 1 Cup will be fine.)

1. Continue to fill the jar with the fresh pureed cabbage/kale, water and Salt as described for the 3 Day Ferment.
2. Let mixture stand at room temperature for 1 day (24 hours).
3. After 1 day (24 hours) has passed the fermenting is completed. Gently stir the mixture and drink (or refrigerate for later use).

The Jilly Juice Protocol has no diet, per se. Eat all available foods.

Shopping List for the Recipe.

a) Cabbage and/or kale

b) Tap Water

c) White Table Salt

d) Measuring cup

e) Tablespoon Salt per batch

f) Blender/Nutribullet/food   processor/knife   (not everyone has electricity)

g) Refrigerator

h) Large <u>glass</u> jars with <u>airtight</u> Lids

i) Glass jar with rubber grommets and locking mechanism no need for coffee filters.

Choosing My Jar(s).

The 2-cup base recipe will fit in a 1-pint jar (16 oz.) or be repeated to fit larger jars like 1-gallon jars or more. This can be any jar from a cleaned out recycled spaghetti sauce jar to a nice Mason jar (Ball jar). The important thing is that I have an airtight lid, and if my lid is uncoated metal (like the two-part Mason jar canning lid) I want to have a coffee filter between the lid and the jar.

Cabbage and Kale.

Cabbage (green or purple) and/or Kale are another personal preference, and it may be one or the other, or any combination of the two. It can be freeze dried powder, frozen or fresh and does not have to be organic. One large head of cabbage yields about 2.5 gallons of juice, so purchase according to how much I choose to make and drink. I have many people asking me why I chose cabbage and kale instead of other vegetables. It was just by happenstance or accidental, yet strategic.

Luckily, both of those vegetables are very dense in nutrition. I originally started using cucumbers to make pickles using the same recipe, but I could not yield enough juice to make it worthwhile. When I tried carrots, I ran into the same issues. I found cabbage and kale to be the easiest to yield large amounts of liquid and so chock full of nutrients along with a diverse food intake.

How to Correct Mistakes When Fermenting.

If I find that I have way more cabbage than water and Salt, then lay off the cabbage and just add the same ratios of water and Salt until I can even out the jar, so it looks 25/50. Let's say for example I forget to put the right amount of Salt and I am already in the middle of the second day of fermentation. Well just add the Salt, mix everything around and then ferment for the next 3 days or more or 24 hours or more, whichever fermentation process I am doing. Let's say I didn't add enough water. What I would do is put everything in a bigger jar, add the right ratios of water, and then ferment for the next 3 days or more or 24 hours or more relative to whatever process I am doing.

Mold

Mold will only happen if my Salt is NOT pure White Table Salt. If I am using mineral Salt, mold thrives on the carbon chemical reaction of minerals and the organic matter from cabbage and kale fermentation when it is exposed to oxygen.

Storage

I can store this juice almost forever. Just make sure everything is below the brine and I mix and check for mold, if I am using mineral (heavy metal) salts because any exposed pieces, even in a sealed environment can still mold while my drink is still fermenting, even in the refrigerator. If I stick to white table Salt, I will not have a major problem with mold or yeast.

Since I am not encouraging anyone to do waterfalls and I really do not want to instruct how people deal with symptoms personally, the main thing is to understand the body's defense systems and how adding ionic energy will help you condition your internal frequencies to align themselves with the external frequencies. It is a slow process. Knowing the triggers of symptoms reside in the feces, this is why I am a fan of the digital release of removing fecal software, so people are not relying on aggressive elements by mouth (the elements hit all the system universally). Like anything, talk to your doctor or become a bootie "pirate"...wink wink. Any treasures you find, goes into the museum of natural history, touché!

Alimentary Canal Pain and
Diaphragmic Digital Release

There are literally 3 lines of defense the body must experience to serve as a warning in an open/closed system before it dies suddenly from overabundance in a closed system.

1. Coughing, sneezing, and mucus with a fever.
2. Diarrhea and vomiting with skin inflammation.
3. Cancer, disease, chronic illness, and autoimmunity.

Why must the person experience the above? In my opinion, the body is exercising its ability to release unwanted entities, so it does not die from overabundance. Once the body exhibits overabundance, it is hard to excommunicate trillions and trillions of colony forming units.

When I first did my own protocol, I already exhibited one or more of the conditions listed below. During my process of release, the preexisting conditions I already had come up for me and I either went to bed and gritted my teeth or I ate a bunch of food to feed the energy. I did not use anything to stop the pain when the pain did get really bad. I am not suggesting everyone should do what I have done, but I figure I would offer my perspective.

If I have questions regarding salt, water, and fermentation, nobody except my doctor should dose how much I should take. As far as salt and dehydration goes, I always drink water and the high blood pressure around salt is also associated with lack of water, causing the anti-diuretic hormone to kick in and retain the water, hence bloating adding more pressure.

Drinking water, regardless, is not a bad idea, not just for bloating, etc.

The following is the list of what I experienced, more or less.

- Acne
- Allergy symptoms
- Ankle, swollen from past sprain
- Anxiety
- Appetite loss
- Back pain
- Barfing, sometimes worms/parasites
- Bloating
- Burping
- Chest congestion
- Chilled feeling
- Cold hands and feet
- Constipation
- Coughing, maybe with green phlegm
- Cystic acne recurrence

- Diarrhea

- Dizziness

- Dry mouth

- Dry skin

- Eye twitch

- Face burning feeling

- Face red

- Farting/gas

- Fatigue/exhaustion

- Fingers tingling

- Flu type symptoms

- Foggy feeling

- Frequent urination

- Growing pains in kids

- Gum/root pain

- Gums burning

- Headache

- Heart palpitations

- Heart racing

- Heartburn

- Hemorrhoids

- Herpes outbreak

- Hot flashes

- Hunger pains/growling stomach

- Increased libido

- Intense emotions

- Itchy skin, scalp, ears, eyes

- Joint pain

- Joint swelling

- Leg Cramps

- Liver pain right side of torso

- Lucid dreams

- Lymph node swelling/pain

- Metal taste in mouth

- Migraines

- Mild chest pain

- Missing organs, limbs, digits, skin grafts, implants

- Mucus from ears

JILLIAN MAI THI BURKE-EPPERLY

- Mucus in throat and nose

- Muscle soreness

- Nausea

- Neck pain

- Ovary pain

- Panic attacks

- Past pain reoccurring for short time

- Pooping parasites

- Rashes

- Runny nose

- Sinus infection

- Sinus pain/pressure

- Sleeplessness

- Sore throat

- Stuffy nose

- Sugar cravings

- Swollen face and eyes

- Swollen hands

- Swollen lymph nodes

- Thirst

- Thrush/white tongue

- Urinary tract infection

- Uterine, sharp pain

- Vomiting

- Weight loss

- Wrist pain

- Zits, expelling yellow/white beads

Every symptom above is the body releasing through energetic pain or proteins of antigen-antibody microbes coming to the surface of the skin on the body. More importantly, these antigen-antibody proteins also get released from the body through my urine, feces, mucus, and all exit points relative to my infections and weaknesses. They could be at the surface of my skin itching or they could induce energy in parts of my body like dull aches or sharp pains. Whenever I have an infection, it will always be torturous like it was for me, as a child.

As a kid, I was highly infected by pinworms in my lower

intestines at the mouth of the anus enough to feel the tickling and poke my little finger to scratch the "itch", only to find little pinworms squirming on my little finger. I was not alarmed, nor told my parents this at the time, but I do remember sitting on the toilet experiencing this. Well, fast forward to 2016, on one hand I was purging the demons (excessive pinworms, et al.) and keeping the "angels", but on the other hand I discovered why I was developing constipation after doing so many waterfalls, or electrolyte saltwater purges/diarrhea with plenty of freshwater backs.

Essentially, the reason why constipation happens is the salt water acts like a cure after it was initially a catalyst, waking up all the different hydra viral antigen-antibody proteins causing aggressive symptoms in some people, like me. Constipation was the outcome of my lower intestine "cured" into suspense thus causing all the bloating and I did not think to drink milk to encourage a mucus build up for release. So, what did I do instead? I used a method called the digital method to understand my own sphincter muscles and pull out the software programming, called feces, holding so many of the conflicting antigen-antibody programming. I would do this every time I felt bloated, backed up, sick from all sorts of symptoms and when I had the worst respiratory problem during the most aggressive time of COVID-19, in 2021. I noticed a correlation of stuffy noses due to my lower intestines full of waste material needing to get out. I also noticed aggressive headaches would stop if I found a way to manually pull out the programming.

Inevitably, I realized, the traditional way of pooping was never going to be my practice anymore and so I have incorporated this non-traditional digital/diaphragmic method of clearing the pipes when my body is full of mucus waste from my defense systems. Constipation comes from the lower intestine cured in suspense until I drank plenty of milk lubricating the exit points allowing for release. All types of cures stop hunger, pain, energy, release, and evolution and over time, cures are deadly. Now I know why I only do JJ a little bit or else trap those aggressive antigen-antibody proteins in my body steadily munching away at my ability to evolve.

In the future, it is expected that once I have expelled the excess antigen-antibody programming and allow deep cellular regeneration, my adaptation process will get easier and easier, despite the changes in the environment. I will always experience periods of adjustment if my environment becomes aggressive or the season changes. However, those who practice sneezing, blowing their nose, etc., will have an easier time than those who do not.

The Power of Suffering with Proper Support

To those who choose not to apply my methods of potential undefined life in an open system and are extremely skeptical of my theories, our perspectives around suffering are extremely different. If I want to apply a belief system no man, woman or child should suffer, then dying suddenly is a blessing for many during climate change. If death is the only answer for suffering then I will see a lot of people dying because the system will not let me suffer, just as I trained the system to take away my pain at the drop of a dime. If people cannot learn how to suffer a little bit or a lot, then death is the only option, to rest in pieces (hydra fragment), and go back to a single celled organism and start over again.

The politics of suffering is such a diverse one that it is another arm of the hydra, metaphorically speaking, and it is an arm worth exploring. It all comes down to that no suffering is death, a little bit of suffering his life, a lot of suffering is retroactive life being released so I only suffer a little bit not a lot, later on when climate will change, yet again. We, as humans living in the first world have been privileged enough to escape vast amounts of suffering with a few wars and issues the last 50 years or so, but we have become so used to not suffering that even a little bit of suffering is unmanageable to all out blasphemy.

Now I am in a world of those who choose to suffer a little bit or a lot, will live, if the suffering is supported properly, or opt out and choose to rest in peace. I just need to make sure that when I am suffering, I am taking responsibility for it, even if I think I was set-up to fail. I definitely am making sure I am not targeting a person, a place or thing to blame for my conditions, because even though I had no choices as a child, as an adult, I now have choices.

The system right now was set up for vast amounts of suffering and many people have a hard time dealing with it, but I actually do not. I suffered a lot throughout my life, so suffering is no stranger to me. If I choose to suffer through the trials and tribulations of life, others will also choose that route, and when it comes to those who should suffer or not suffer, let the system be the one to determine who suffers a lot and who suffers a little.

The Jilly Juice and I represents just one hydra arm that can handle the suffering because I was primed for it. Little did I know my childhood was getting me ready for this time and it is natural and expected to "hate" my childhood if I were groomed for so much potential in the future. However, at some point, if I happen to survive my childhood, my adulthood and even midlife, I have every opportunity to develop the next phase of my life when coming upon the fork in the road. And so this is what my mom meant; when I care about somebody and I know how aggressive life will be, I will make sure my children are prepared for the world they will be entering into.

Peace and energy. May the odds be in my favor.

PS

Keep an eye out for my next book. At the end of this simulation, entering into the next phase, humans and animals can literally give birth to themselves every day if they train their bodies to evolve with the environment. In this environment of 2022, if a human wanted to give birth to themselves, it would be extremely painful if they do not understand the process.

Printed in the United States
by Baker & Taylor Publisher Services